50 Sha
More Poems & P.

MW00893572

By: Howard B. Altman

Dedication

This is for my parents, Stewart and Emily Altman. Your love, values, and combination of whimsy and black humor made this book possible. Thank you for all your encouragement and support, and for never yelling at me no matter where my (inherited) creative streak took me. Not even when I broke the blender trying to invent the pureed Halloween candy shake.

Introduction

We are two years aboard the Trump Train(wreck). Mar-a-Lard-Ass a/k/a Burrito Mussolini a/k/a Crappy Gilmore a/ka the Kumquat Pol Pot remains an arrogant, bloated, bullying, seditious, simpleminded, syphilitic, treasonous, traitorous, tiny-handed tyrant. So, I wrote more poems and parodies to keep from crying.

Like *Goodnight, Loon*, this is a mix of parodies and poems. If prefaced by "Song Break", sing along to the song parodied, preferably aloud. The others in the waiting room will thank you. If not prefaced by "Song Break", it's a poem, and you can make up your own melody. It's fun!

A note on formatting: Lyrics/poems are mine. Typos are Siri's.

<u>Opening Limericks</u>

Tiny hands tweet in a rage
'Bout Google, the Press, Carter Page.
I must say, it is fun
See him coming undone.
Can't wait till he's put in a cage.

Common sense, Don can't seem to absorb it.
Educate him? I am all for it.
But he can't even read.
So Space Force, do the deed:
Make the dolt the first orange in orbit.

There once was a fat orange traitor
Who wanted to be a dictator.
Each word is a crock.
And he's dumb as a rock.
Impeach the fool sooner than later.

Patriotic Songs

Trump sings America the Beautiful

O beautiful bodacious guys.
Hamburger ways and reign.
For diet cokes & Burger King
Aboard my private plane.
America, America it is all about ME!
With misspelled tweets from toilet seats.
I want my KFC.

Don sings God Bless America

God bless America.
Land that I'm from.
May pal Paulie
Says they'll maul me.
As I tweet misspelled lies with my thumbs.
I am frightened.
They indicted.
All my comrades turning tail.
God bless America.
I'll go to jail.
God bless America.
I'll go to jail.

A Poem:

Lacking in reason.
Stinking of treason.
Stutter & stammer
O'er 2nd grade grammar.
Orange & vomitus.
Can't say "anonymous".
No one can teach him.
Let's hope they impeach him.
The traitorous chump
Who is Donald Trump.

Song Break: To Another Brick in the Wall
Trump don't want no education.
Trump likes FoxNews thought control.
Arming teachers in the classroom.
Trump he just is Putin's clone.
(Hey! Trumpy! You are Putin's clone!)
All in all he's just another jerk with no wall.

A Goodnight Poem

Goodnight Twitter, now the liar
Rants that he did not conspire.
And backs it with conspiracy peddling
That Russia had no role in meddling.
Don also tried to break EU
Cause that's what Putin said to do.
Hey Donny, you so love the tsar?
Don't came back from SSR.

Song Break: To Mr. Tambourine Man
(Dedicated to @Chownart)

<u>Chorus</u>:

Hey Mr. Tangerine Man
Treason's a felony.
You are guilty and there ain't no one believing you.
Hey Mr. Tangerine man
Guilty as can be.
Come midterm elections
Mueller's coming for you.

You're an ignorant and racist fool
A lying raving swine.
You should be doing time.
Your admin is a crime.
But you're still tweeting.

Your ignorance amazes me.
As you sit and tweet
From your toilet seat.
You think Mueller will quit you must be dreaming.

(Repeat Chorus)

You act like you're the orange king
Of your dictatorship.
Stop whining, get a grip. Get off the ego trip.
The good will of our allies you've been sqanderin'.
Let's boot you on your derriere to history you'll fade
You want you own parade, your term is a charade.
Resign and go away and we'll be dancing.

(Repeat Chorus)

Song Break: To Carry on My Wayward Son (for Don Jr.)

Carry on my traitor son.
There'll be jail and you are done.
A plea bargain would be best.
Don't you lie no more.

Even Bannon knows the meeting was treason.
Traitor Tot don't know the trouble that he's in.
No one buys into your lies, man
That daddy didn't know.
Fredo better buy a clue or a notion.
Maybe borrow from Scott Pruitt some lotion.
Soon in prison you'll be squealing.
You will hear the warden say:

Carry on my traitor son.
There'll be jail and you are done.
A plea bargain would be best.
Don't you lie no more.

<u>Poem Time</u>!

I think that I shall never see
A man as stupid as DT.
A man who panders to dumb herds
And Capitalizes Random Words.
Who knows not grammar, English, spelling
Yet spends his days whining and yelling.
How I wish that we could dump
The orange traitor they call Trump.

Your skin it is orange.
Your hands they are tiny.
You're ignorant, racist, stupid & whiny.
You're like a child, a toddler, maybe
With such tiny hands who whines like a baby.
Google's not "rigged", nor the press, CNN.
It's just you're a traitor who belongs in the Pen.

Song Break: To the oldie, King of the Road

Traitor for sale or rent.
Spreading lies & discontent.
Those lies he loves to tell
Buy an eight by eight jail cell.
He's got no brains, no common sense.
Don't know who's worse, he or Pence.
A mean of treason.
He's an old bloated load.

Traitor for sale or rent.
Golfs with taxes money spent.
All mirrors, lies & smoke.
Guzzles the Diet Coke.
Scarfing the KFC
Treason, lies & felony.
No valid POTUS, notice. Fat bloated load.

No heart, no soul, no brain.
Porta-potty called "Trump Train".
Orange of hair and face.
Every word a big disgrace.
He ate each Big Mac he had found.
Now he's 80 feet around.
No valid POTUS, notice, fat bloated load.

Traitor for sale or rent.
Fat orange malcontent.
Can't think, can't read, can't spell.
Oh Donny go to hell.
Corrupt, deluded slime.
Can't go a day without committing a crime.
He's a man of treason
He's an old bloated load.

Headline: Trump again attacks the NFL players kneeling to protest racial inequality. Also, Michael Cohen pleads guilty and offers to cooperate with Special Counsel.

Goodnight Poem

Goodnight Twitter, what a feeling.
Trump obsessed again with kneeling.
Tariff plan has gone to hell.
But, he says the NFL!
Cohen about to spill the beans.
So rant about the football teams.
Putin still his bestest bud.
NATO, allies, all a dud.
Mueller knocking at the door.
That's what his distraction's for.

Song Break: To The Pina Colada Song

If you like treasonous dotards
Ranting fools with no brain.
Like obstruction of justice.
For the law have disdain.
If you love random tweets at midnight.
If you aren't too bright.
Then you likely are MAGA
Pray to God they indict.

Song Break: To Only the Good Die Young
(Dedicated to Dani Sage)

Come on Bob Mueller don't make us wait.
Indict the fat traitor before it's too late.
We're tired of seeing him whine and dictate.
Tweeting lies with his thumbs.
Indict the orange bum.
That's what I said.
Indict the orange bum.

Bridge:

He's got an orange face
And a Russian owned affiliation.
He's a fat Al Capone.
Perched on his gaudy throne.
Donny Jr. shoulda' said no.
When he got the Russian invitation.
It is a crime you see.
Guilty of felony, whoah-oh-oh.

So come on Bob Mueller don't make us wait.
Indict the fat traitor before it's too late
Get the Grand Jury, no need for debate.
Time that the sin's undone.
Indict the orange bum.

Song Break: To Beat It

A racist bully so obnoxious & rude.
But every time you tweet we know you did collude.
Keep it up, Don and you're gonna be screwed.
So tweet it. Just tweet it.

You orange moron always tweeting out lies.
Crushing your gold toilet with those thunder thighs.
With every word you say the charade you sell dies.
So tweet it. Just tweet it.

Chorus:

Tweet it. Just tweet it. Tweet out lies & hate
Repeat it.
Inane, insipid, dimwit uncouth.
Your phone would break if you told the truth.
But tweet it. Just tweet it.

Await the date that your kleptocracy ends.
You sit around the house just watching
Fox&Friends.
Scarfing Big Macs in your plus-size Depends.
But tweet it.

Bridge

Oh you tweet that its SAD but tweet it. Tweet it.
Watch the MAGA morons bleat it.
Tweet NO COLLUSION each day and night.
It does not matter you're not too bright, just tweet it.

Trump National Anthem

O say did they pee on a mattress that night?
Oh the Russia lies failed.
Reelection hope's fleeting.
He's beholden to tsars & his grammar's a fright.
All the BS we read
In misspelled late night tweeting.
Oh the bright orange hair & the Stormy affair.
Watching FoxNews all night in XL underwear.
Oh say does that dumb orange moron still rave.
About the crimes he did commit
And the Big Mac he craves.

Song Break! To Officer Krupke (from West Side Story)

Gee kindly Robert Mueller
You gotta understand.
I didn't tweet obstruction.
It's just my tiny hands.
With all my fake denials.
You know I did collude.
Goodness, gracious that's why I am screwed.

Gee Fat Orange Trumpy
We're very upset.
You haven't been impeached.
Or just resigned as of yet.
You're just a dumb Klansman
Who took off the hood.
Deep down inside you're just no good.
(Just no good!)
You're no good, You're no good,
You're no earthly good.
On the best of days you're no damn good!

The trouble he's lazy.
The trouble is he lies.
The trouble is he's crazy.
"It's fake news!" he cries
The trouble is his tweeting.
The trouble, he's a chump.
But the biggest problem: he is Trump.
Gee, fat orange Trumpy we're begging you please.
Your tweeting only proves
You've got a mental disease.
Gee, fat orange Trumpy, What are we to do?
Gee, fat orange Trumpy, Trump you!

Ode to Dotard Don

His mind is declining.
He cannot stop whining.
For daughter he's pining.
I wish he's resigning.
Blames Dems and the Press
For his godawful mess.
Making sense less & less.
Oh impeach, it'd #BeBest.

Song Break: To Desperado
(Dedicated to Sam Kirkham)

Desperate Donald.
Why don't you come to your senses.
Even Mike Pence is
Ashamed of your crime.
You are a felon.
Although you thought that you hid it.
Mike Cohen did admit it.
You're gonna' do time.

You're shouting "No Collusion!"
At your inbred MAGA love-in.
But Donny, lying's always been your sin.
If this probe is a "witch hunt"
Your campaign it is a coven.
And day-by-day Mueller's closing in.

Desperate Donald.
Why don't you come to your senses.
You're out of defenses.
We know you're a fraud.
You're a liar, though peeing hookers excite you.
When Muller indicts you
We're gonna' applaud.

Ode to Orange

Oh orange moron lacking in reasoning.
Sending his day lying & treasoning.
Anything decent, and Cheeto will soil it.
Tweeting his hate from the seat of his toilet.
Hate of the Press, of the Dems & all races.
There is no end to Donny's disgraces.
Congress, if you want to give us a gift,
We'd like an Amendment: by name, 25th.

Song Break:
I can see Clearly Now The Rain is Gone

I can see clearly now your brain is gone.
The men with straight jackets are on the way.
They'll use the 25th amendment, Don.
Oh it will be a bright, bright,
Impeach-y day.

Mar-a-Lard-Ass again is rage-tweeting.
Cause he knew about Traitor-Tot's meeting.
So he'll lie and distract,
But it won't change the fact
Time in office is soon to be fleeting.

Crying "witch hunt", manic, hyper.
Someone needs to change his diaper.
Soon the spoiled baby Don
Will go to jail, or just be gone.

Song Break: To Hey Jude
(Dedicated to @NickiKnowsNada)

"Fake News", tweets tiny hands.
"It's a witch hunt!" he'll whine and stammer.
A pile of barely literate mass.
Trump couldn't pass his grade school grammar.

"Fake News", he tweets each day.
"No Collusion!" he'll cry & stammer.
But Mueller reads every word that he pens.
He's going to send
Trump to the slammer.

So, any time he sends a tweet
You know he's beat.
He rants and he raves in his denial.
For well we know that he's insane.
He has no brain.
The KFC grease made him senile.
(na na na na na na na na).

"Fake News", tweets tiny hands.
The complexion of year-old cheddar.
An angry, whiny, litany of lies.
He can't disguise
WITH CAPS LOCKED LETTERS
LETTERS, LETTERS, LETTERS
LETTERS, LETTERS
Ahhhhhhhhh!
Na, na, na na, na na, na
Na, na, na, na, Fake News!

Song Break: To Lido Shuffle
(Dedicated to Dvora Koelling)

Cheeto is a moron and a lying sack.
We wish he'd go to Russia, never to come back.
He's a two-bit czar.
Orange hair bizarre.
An idiot.
A ranting, raving moron, redefines "unfit".

Orange ass-clown.
Can't wait till he's going down, Putin's clone.
Must give Bob Woodward credit.
Think you're free, Don, forget it.
You bloated load.

Cheeto
Whoah.
He's going down, treason you know.
Cheeto, you moron, you gotta go.
Cheeto.
Whoah.
Donny, oh let us teach you.
Resign or we'll impeach you.
Don hit the road.

Song Break: To We Didn't Start the Fire
Co-written by Sam Kirkham

Fired AG Sally Yates.
Others soon met similar fates,
Michael Flynn and Katie Walsh.
Sean Spicer would be gone
Omoarosa screams and shouts
Soon she was escorted out.
Priebus out Kelly in.
The Ferris wheel goes on.

Chorus

All the folks Trump did hire.
They were all conspiring.
Or victims of firing.
All the folks Trump did hire.
Every job they blew it.
Like Pollution Pruitt.

Gary Cohn, Hope Hicks,
Stormy Daniels turning tricks.
Tillerson and Manafort.
Soon he saw his day in court.
Gorka, Bannon new alt-right,
Trumps says "Nazis, they're alright"
Comey, Pruitt, Robert Porter Scaramucci Goodbye

(Repeat Chorus)

<u>Ode to Seditious Sycophants</u>

I can't stand morons Diamond & Silk.
Lou Dobbs, Ptomaine Lahren, & all of their ilk.
Lying & Deep State & two-minute hate.
Like Putin & Kim, Don wants to dictate.
What I wouldn't give to not hear him yammer.
And tweet out his lies in improper grammar.
It's just a cult of dimwitted clods.
Who drank the KoolAid & ate the Tide Pods.

Song Break: America the Beautiful (for Don Jr.)

O Traitor Tot, you Russian bot.
Your Twitter feed's all lies.
You rant and rave, insult the Left.
But met with Russian spies.
America, America, Don Jr. betrayed thee.
The traitor boy played Putin's ploy.
And that's a felony.

Poems for Don's Trade War

Goodnight Twitter. Goodnight, loon.
It seems we'll lose his trade war soon.
Car prices up, and gas prices too.
Don tweeting lies from his overstressed loo.
Traitorous moron, ignorant ass.
Dumb as a brick, fat as Mama Cass.
Don is failure as dumb as can be.
Should be in jail for his felony.

Trump you run your lying trap.
While selling made in China crap.
At rallies & your darn Trump Store.
All while waging your trade war.
Costs us jobs every day.
To please Russia & NK.
You just do a tyrant's bidding.
"America first", Don? You must be kidding.

Song Break: To Simon & Garfunkel's
The Sounds of Silence
(This appeared in Goodnight Loon, but I was told
it's a favorite, so here 'tis)

Sitting watching FOX&Friends.
Wearing nothing but Depends.
They all know that Don Jr. lied
About the meeting he tried to hide.
Now the cries for impeachment
Echo through the Senate halls.
Justice calls.
You'll hear the sound of sirens.

And the people bowed and prayed.
For the country you betrayed.
Oh how Mueller will teach you.
Traitor Don they will impeach you.
You can tweet your drivel from your cell.
Go to hell.
You'll hear the sound of sirens.

Goodnight Poem

Goodnight Twitter, ladies men.
A dotard rally, yet again.
Harley's moving, Mueller probe.
Anger all round the globe.
So Donny self-congratulate.
"Tell me MAGA ain't I great."
Donny you corrupted waste.
I don't care about your base.
Stop blowing dollars on this crap.
In short, moron, shut your trap.

Song Break: To Day Tripper

He commits treason.
He colludes with Russian spies.
He commits treason.
Then he tweets his outright lies.
He is a big traitor.
Treason weasel, yeah.
Take Mueller not long to find out.
Yeah he'll find out.

He's a big sleaze. Taking bribes from ZTE.
He's a big sleaze. Hope we'll have his guilty plea.
He is a big traitor.
Treason weasel, yeah.
Take Mueller not long to find out.
Yeah he'll find out.

<u>Headline</u>: Red Hen Restaurant asks Sarah Sanders to leave. She complains about it from her government-issued Twitter account.

A poem for Huckleberry:

Let's do what Sarah H can't do:
Like say something wholly true.
Or grab a meal at the Red Hen.
Or love thy neighbor, count to 10.
Or not use your Press position
To bitch about your meal omission.
Go a day not saying "witch hunt".
Or not being a feckless (person).

Song Break: To U2's Desire

Lordy. All the crap he tweets.
Misspelled frights from his toilet seat.
Pathologic. He's a liar.
Conspire.

Went to Russia
Where the paid hookers peed.
Putin taped it.
Now he pays for the deed.
He'll grant favors.
He'll deny it.
It's as real
As his KFC diet.
Owned by Putin
That orange liar
Conspire.
Conspire.

Headline: Trump holds another useless rally
(though no one is up for election) in North Dakota

Goodnight Twitter, the fat load a'
Rallying in North Dakota.
Market tanks & kids in pens.
Hold a "love me" fest again.
The only way Trump spends his time.
Are these dumb rallies on our dime.
Orwellian 2-hour hate.
Watch the moron lie, berate
allies & the racist elf.
Treason rat, go FOX yourself.

Song Break: To Love Stinks

He wants her.
But she's his kin.
He says "You look like my daughter".
Incest's a sin.

His every word
A dirty lie.
Some slept with Trump.
Don't ask me why.

All of us hope he ends up in the clink.
One thing for sure: Trump stinks.
Trump stinks (Trump stinks) yeah yeah.
Trump stinks yeah yeah.

<u>Headline</u>: Trump plans a summit with Putin where only the 2 of them will be present, with no witnesses. Because, of course he will.

So Trump will ask Vlad to come visit.
Not really his best idea, is it?
It's like open season
For GOP treason.
Come elections, tell them where to kiss it.

Song Break: I'm a Little Teapot

I am a stable genius, fat and stout.
Hear me whine and see me pout.
Watch me praising Putin all about.
Vote the lying traitors out.

Song Break: To Bruno Mars's Grenade
(Dedicated to Science Based Cathe)

Tiny thumbs, there you go.
You are gonna' tweet, oh.
Lies, lies, lies each day.
From your toilet seat.
Should have known you were dumb
From your first speech.
"Islands have big water"
Pining for your daughter.

You are owned by Vlad.
Your followers are trash.
Your followers are trash, inbred brain-dead gits.
Bilking MAGA morons, taking all their cash.
For your MAGA red hat biz.

You know you've been played MAGA.
His promises, a charade MAGA .
You know you'll never get laid MAGA.
He won't a thing for ya'.
Oh, no.

It seems you all have no brain.
That, or you're just insane.
Cause that fat orange baby.
Will bring you all shame.

A Morning Poem

Morning, Twitter and fat Nixon.
Did he get his FoxNews fix in?
Whining that the rest's fake news.
Donny you are bound to lose.
All you touch, an epic fail.
Fake probe? Manafort's in jail.
For you to join him we're all rootin.
So go cry to your buddy Putin.

Song Break: To Elton John's Tiny Dancer
(Dedicated to April M)

Orange baby.
Fat and lazy.
Tubby and spray-tanned.
Fat and vile.
He's senile .
Clearly is Putin's man.
Stupid wiener.
Dim demeanor
Panders to the Klan.
And now he's tweeting.
Always bleating.
Tiny phone in tiny hands.

Scarfing a Happy Meal.
Perched on his giant rear.
Only glue can hold his hairpiece.
So Vlad says softly, slowly.

Hold me close, O Tiny-Handed
Think "Ivanka" during foreplay.
Let us cast our lot in treason.
Commit felonies today.

Song Break: To Genesis Invisible Touch

When he is campaigning
For a candidate
They lose by a landslide.
His thumbs up seals their fate.
And now they know
Trump is an albatross.
His endorsement just seals a loss.
Now it seems they're running, running from him.
Trumpy he has a reverse Midas touch.
He makes a choice and soon it's falling apart.
Trumpy he has a reverse Midas touch.
No "winning" here just losing raised to an art.

Poem time:

Orange, rotund, yellow-haired, tiny-handed.
Corrupt, a crook, Putin-bought & FOX-branded.
Oh we'd rejoice if only he landed
In the Federal Pen
For his crimes there remanded.

Song Break: To Wouldn't That be Loverly (My Fair Lady)

For my best friend and "older brother", Mark Plavin

Sitting round on his derriere.
They forgot to alert daycare.
Oh, that bright orange hair,
Oh, wouldn't that be Trumperly.

Lots of Big Macs for him to eat.
Tweeting lies from his toilet seat.
"He's great", the MAGA bleat
Oh, wouldn't that be Trumperly?

Trump committed a felony.
Just as guilty as he can be.
Oh won't you please impeach?
Oh, wouldn't that be Trumperly?

His skin it is orange.
His hands they are teeny.
The ignorant, racist, rotund Mussolini.
His badly spelled tweets, he cannot be taught.
But Putin just proved that he can be bought.
But Mueller will give reason to be excited
Come the probe's end, we'll see Trump indicted.

Song Break: To Hotel California
(Dedicated to @GirlNamedBoston)

Golfing at Mar-a-largo. Dyed bright orange hair.
Warm smell of burritos rising up through the air.
Cozies up to the Russians
For a lobbyist thing.
Treason's full-time employment.
Prez a hobbyist thing.

Welcome to the Hotel Mar-a-Largo.
Such an awful place. Such an orange face.
Plenty of goons at the Hotel Mar-a-Largo
All the Russian spies selling alibis.

Gaudy gold-plated ceiling.
Diet Coke on ice.
He says, "we will all be prisoners, soon".
10-to-life will suffice.
And still I'm begging & pleading to Chris Wray.
Use the back door for my perp walk
Or I'll here them all say:

Welcome to the Hotel Mar-a-Largo.
Such an awful place. Such an orange face,
Plenty of goons at the Hotel Mar-a-Largo.
All the Russian spies selling alibis.

Headline: Tomi "Ptomaine" Lahren rails against immigrants, complains that they "don't learn English." Then, it is revealed that her grandparents are immigrants who never learned to speak English.

Goodnight Twitter O the barren
Vapid mind of Ptomaine Lahren.
Spewing hate o'er immigration.
Panders to Fox racist nation.
Tammy it is illustrative
That your family isn't native.
Tammy you did not distinguish
Granny never did speak English.
Tammy you're a hypocrite.
A lying vapid piece of poop.

Song Break! To Hair

Look at that awful hair, bright orange hair.
Tarnished, varnished, colored & spray painted.
Flyaway orange hair (hair!), flappin' on the tarmac.
Dye, baby, crybaby, oh how he lies bout his hair!
Thinning, spinning, how is all that #winning.
Trump hair.

Song Break: To Space Oddity (In honor of
Trump's Space Force)

This is Ground Control to Major Trump
You really are an fool.
And the people want to see you thrown in jail.
Booted out of here on your fat orange tail.
Here he is tweeting from a bedpan
Traitor of the world
Mueller comes for you
And there's nothing you can do.

Headline: NRA picks Ollie North as its president.
Yes, the same guy who sold arms to the enemy.

The NRA will sally forth
With Iran-Contra's Ollie North.
Anyone could have predicted
They would pick a prez convicted.
More GOP values yellin'
From their stock convicted felon.
Seems the GOP's one vision:
Appoint those who've been to prison.

Song Break: To Elvis's Don't Be Cruel

We know he can be found
Sitting on the throne.
Tweeting false denials
From his telephone.
Orange fool, all you say's true.

Don's in trouble bad. (bop bop).
In over his orange head. (bop bop).
He is owned by Vlad. (bop bop).
He taped em peeing on the bed. (bop bop).
Orange fool, all you say's true.
We don't want no "witch hunt" tale.
Donny, we just want you thrown in jail.

<u>Headline</u>:   Reports surface that Trump *twice* asked
Bill Gates to explain the difference between HIV
and HPV to him.

Goodnight Twitter gals & mates.
Seems that Donnie asked Bill Gates
Was AIDS was the same as HPV
Seems Dotard has an STD.
Franklin Graham, oh Christian born again,
Don hath slept with stars of porn again.
Seems Trump in a rare confession
Wants more than just voter suppression.

Song Break: If I Only had a Brain

I'd defend myself from treason.
Or give a valid reason.
For my Russian-bought campaign.
I'd be more than a dullard
Tellin' lies 'bout Robert Muller.
If I only had a brain.

I'd send tweets with proper grammar.
Instead of lie & yammer.
My tweets cause teachers pain.
But I'd know I'd get a bootin
For conspirin' with Putin,
If you only had a brain.

: Trump invites Kim Kardashian to the
White House to discuss prison reform.

Goodnight Twitter, goodnight all.
Now old Trumpy had a ball.
Met Kim K on prison biz.
The only bigger ass than his.
Sought tips on prison rape reduction.
For when he's sent up for obstruction.
The day he's jailed will be exquisite.
Where his friend Roseanne can visit.

Song Break: To Manic Monday
(Dedicated to @DonnaIsack)

6:00 already Don is sitting down to send a tweet.
Tweeting "No Collusion!"
From 40-inch wide toilet seat.
The man we hate
How I hope another country would trade.
But from his tweets it is clear of Mueller he is afraid
It's just another Panicked Monday.
What'd his dimwit son say?
Can't wait until he's done, hey
It's just another Panicked Monday.

: In advance of the G7 meeting, Trump attacks each ally and praises Putin.

Dear G7,

We'd trade you a Trump for Trudeau or Macron.
We'd trade for Merkel or for leaders unknown.
We'd trade him for schnitzel or bangers & mash.
We'd trade him for nada or unwanted trash.
We'd trade for your worst whatever you had.
Oh, screw it: just take him. Return him to Vlad.

Song break! To Gimme Some Lovin'

Well the moron is tweeting
"No collusion" and more.
Keeps whining "it's a witch hunt".
Man this fool is a bore.
Whining like a baby, but his lies are for naught.
Cause Mueller's getting closer.
Don will be caught.

And I hate you traitor.
I hate you traitor.

If it's a witch hunt,

Your campaign's a coven!
(your campaign is a coven)
Your campaign's a coven!.
(your campaign is a coven)
Your campaign's a coven!
Everyday!

Trump tweets are like daily turds.
Drivel via misspelled words.
Whiny, nasty daily lies.
random Words To capitalize.
Colored like a wilted carrot.
Repeating BS like a parrot.
Witch hunt, Hillary, No Collusion.
Everyday a Don delusion.
Don "won big decision"?
Don, you cannot tweet from prison.

Song Break: To Beach Boys' Fun Fun Fun

He's a fat, whiny, orange, lying
Putin-loving criminal traitor.
Tweeting threats to our allies.
Kissing up to a Korean dictator.
All the country'd like to say
"Adios Don, we won't see you later".
Yes you'll be done, done, done
Soon Bob Mueller's gonna put you away.

Birthday poems for the traitor (6/14/18)

Crappy birthday Putin stooge.
Mueller's present will be Yuge.
He's revoking Paulie's bail.
After hearings, he's in jail.
Like rats aboard a sinking ship
This MAGA rat is sure to flip.
Crappy birthday go to hell.
Next one's in a prison cell.

To help you mark your birth date
Here are ways to celebrate:
Donny it may BeBest
Watching Mike Cohen's arrest.
Or make a visit to the court
Revoking bail of Manafort.
Don, a celebration fine
Would be if you would just resign.

Song Break: To Another One Bites the Dust
(Dedicated to @SchoolIlluminati)

Mike Cohen walks into the room.
NDA is ready go.
He'll pay you not to say you did the deed.
With his boss in ol' Moscow.

Cash or credit, are you listening, Miss?
It's an offer that you cannot refuse.
Cause if you get the word out he's sleeping around
He is sure to lose.

Dum dum dum…
Another one paid by Trump.
Dum dum dum…
Another one paid by Trump.
And another porn star and another porn star
Another one paid by Trump.
Hey, he's gonna sleep with you.
Another one paid by Trump.

<u>Headline</u>: June 15, 2018. The NY Attorney General
sues the Trump Foundation for fraud.

NY brought a birthday suit
Against your phony institute.
NY AG's birthday gift
A suit, cause grifters gotta grift.
MAGA fools may be perplexed.
Keep whining, Don, for Mueller's next.

Song Break: My Favorite Things

Clandestine meetings held in Trump Towers.
Paid Russian hookers who give golden showers.
Diet Cokes, Big Macs & KFC wings.
These are a few of Don's favorite things.

It's a Witch Hunt! No Collusions!
All that he can say.
We wish he'd just take his favorite things
And go the heck away.

To the Byrds Turn, Turn, Turn

Michael will turn, turn, turn, turn.
Trump commits treason, turn, turn, turn.
A racist moron, an IQ of 11.
Watch Donny whine, watch Donny lie.
A Russian plant, a Putin spy.
An incompetent moron, an epic fail.
For all our peace, please put his butt in jail.

Song Break: To I Guess That's Why They Call it the Blues

They'll put Trump away.
He won't be the prez forever.
Worst that we had.
I can honestly say Nixon was probably better.
But there on TV, lies every night do not help.
And more than ever.
I simply know you
Are just State news and nothing else.

I guess that's why they call it FoxNews.
Lies on the air, it is all that you do.
Ranting blonde morons, Nunes conspires.
Panders to nazis and treasonous liars.
And I guess that's why they call it FoxNews.

Songs for Paul Manafort

I Fought the Law
Paul fought the law & the law won.
Paul fought the law & the law won.
Paul fought the law & the law won.
Paul fought the law & the law won.

Witness tampering, lies spun.
Paul fought the law & the law won.
Paul fought the law & the law won.

He and Team Treason broke the law with Vlad.
House arrest is done.
Bigliest treason that we ever had.
Paul fought the law & the law won.
Paul fought the law & the law won.

Jailhouse Rock

Had to do a week at the county jail.
Manafort was there looking scared & pale.
MAGA threw a tantrum Donny here's the thing:
Manafort's a tool but he's gonna sing.
No shock, oh no Donny no shock
After pimping for the Eastern Bloc.
Manafort is gonna talk.

Song Break: Little Star

Tweet on tweet on pawn to tsar.
Putin put you where you are.
Every day you rant and lie.
Blame the Press & phony spies.
Tweet on tweet on pawn to tsar.
Soon you'll be put behind bars.

Song Break! To Son of a Preacher man

Stephen Miller's the devil's spawn.
Brought from the depths when Trump came along.
Stevie knew what the vile base meant.
So they unchained him from the basement.
Bald head and rodent eyes.
Oh no, it's no surprise.

He's not a man, just an evil bot, see.
And he's called Steven Miller, man.
The only bald head & bug-eyed Nazi.
And he's called Steven Miller, man.

: June 18, 2018: Trump officially creates a
Space Force, and Kirjsten "with a silent J" Neilsen
refuses to apologize for caging immigrant babies
and tearing them from their families because, she
says, "immigrants break the law".

Goodnight Twitter. Goodnight stars.
I wish Don was behind bars.
Along with Krijsten with a "J".
Let's put all of them away.
Hate the child love the egg.
Try these morons in The Hague.
Send them to the moon of course.
To join in Donny's new Space Force.
Send them anyplace but here.
Vote them out by next year.

Song Break: To Stand By Me

When he's in Moscow.
Plotting with the czar.
And they tape him
As he's watching hookers pee.
Vlad said he hid the tape.
And he'll still hide the tape.
Just as long as Don commit felonies.
Oh Donny, Donny
Felony.
Oh, felony.
Treason, lies.
Russian spies.
Felonies.

<u>Headline</u>: Corey Lewandowski goes on the news to mock a 10 year old immigrant girl with Down Syndrome who was torn from her mother: 'womp, womp' he said.

Song Break: To Brady Bunch Theme

Here's a Corey likes to beat his lady.
Doesn't mind mocking kidnapped girls.
He's vile lying thug just like Sarah.
He should be sporting pearls.
Here's a Corey & he's pretty shady.
He likes mocking kids with Down Syndrome.
He's no grown man, just a lying traitor.
He's missing chromosomes.

Then one day old Corey met the Donald.
He brought him some KFC for lunch.
They joined up & committed treason.
That's they way they all became the treason bunch.
The treason bunch, the treason bunch.
That's the way they became the treason bunch.

June 20, 2018: Trump signs an Executive Order temporarily ending ripping immigrant kids from their parents. To celebrate, he holds another pointless "tell me how great I am" rally on our dime, this time in Duluth.

I will not watch you in Duluth.
I will not watch you maul the truth.
I will not watch you on TV.
Gaseous bag of felony.
I will not watch you praising Kim.
Low IQ Don so dim.
I will not watch you rally hate.
Boast of how you can dictate.
I'll turn on a TV station
To tune in for your resignation.

Song Break: Oompa Loompa time!

Oompa Loompa dupity do.
You commit crimes Mueller's coming for you.
Oompa Loompa dupity dee.
Obstruction of justice is a felony.
What do you do with a racist old fool?
Orange, illiterate KGB tool.
What do you do with a traitorous whale?
You throw his fat ass in jail.
Cause he is a traitor.

Oompa Loompa dupity dum.
Don is as orange as citrus come.
Oompa Loompa dupity durk.
Why are we stuck with this fat orange jerk?
What do you do when they're onto your lies.
Make up some more about Democrat spies.
When all the lies start to come apart fast.
Manafort will flip at last.
You will go to prison.

Song Break: to Layla!

What'll you do when Mueller's coming?
Manafort is gonna flip.
Don't you see
Your pals are gonna flee.
Just like rats aboard a ship.
Traitor!
They'll have you on your knees.
Traitor!
Your mind is so diseased.
Traitor!
Better cut your losses and resign.

No use in procrastination.
Even MAGAtts know you'll fail.
Orange hue.
Calls people "low IQ".
But moron, you will go to jail.
Traitor!
Tyrants meet bad ends.
Traitor!
Don't count on Fox&Friends.
Traitor!
Can't wait for the day you're doing time.

Song Break: to Danny Boy

Oh Donny Boy, indictments they are coming.
From Flynn to Cohen, guilty pleas applied.
Your fixer's gone, and Mueller know you're lying.
To jail you go, oh kiss your butt goodbye.

Song Break: To Let it Be

When I find myself at night in Moscow
Russian hookers come to me.
Paid by buddy Putin.
Let 'em pee.
Though I'm now beholden
There is a tape that they can't see.
From my night in Moscow.
Let 'em pee.
Let 'em pee, let 'em pee, let 'em pee, let 'em pee.
Treason is the answer.
Let 'em pee.

And when the wife looks dowdy
There are prostitutes that wait for me.
Hide the tape tomorrow.
Let 'em pee.
I wake up to the sound of Putin
"Peepee Tape", he threatens me.
Speaking words of whiz, dumb.
Let 'em pee.
Let 'em pee, let 'em pee, let' em pee, let 'em pee.
Treason is my answer.
Let 'em pee.

And when all of Bob Mueller's people
Studying the probe agree.
Don should go to prison.
Let it be.
Though he may be pardoned
That's for the next prez to see.
Mueller is the answer.
Let 'em pee.
Let 'em pee, let 'em pee, let 'em pee, let 'em pee.
Mueller is the answer.
Let 'em pee.

70

Song Break: To Yellow Polka Dot Bikini

Oh he wanted to sleep with his daughter.
Oh, all the gross things he'd say.
He couldn't go out with his daughter.
So, porn star proxies OK.
2, 3, 4, Don is a perverted boor.

He was a lying racist orange meanie.
Tiny-handed Mussolini.
Oh we wish that he'd just go away.
A lying racist orange meanie
Tiny-handed Mussolini.
For his impeachment each of us pray.

To Back in the USSR
(Dedicated to @Pookietooth)

Sitting in a bathrobe watching Fox&Friends.
Can't spell special "council" right.
Lying and the self-obsession never ends.
Twitter feed's a dreadful fright.
Collude with the USSR.
Donny's in bed with the Czar, boy.
Collude with the USSR.

Headline: June 30, 2018: Justice Kennedy retires, Trump to make his USSC pick over the 4th of July weekend.

Whoever's Don Supreme Court pick
Is guaranteed to make me sick.
It could be incept shrill and obscene
Vile not-a-judge-Jeanine.
Or the man of choice for Donny
Could be nutty Giuliani.
Whoever orange moron chooses
Likely racked up law abuses.
Joe Arpaio, Pruitt scum
Donny chooses only bums.

Song Break: To Dancing Queen
(Dedicated to @SueinRockville)

Lindsey hopes voter turnout's low.
Looking out for fit to throw.
Now he caters to Putin.
Praising him in that drawl.
Lindsey can have a ball.
Anyone could predict his mess.
Dressed in J. Edgar Hoover's dress.
Now he caters to Putin.
Lying ignorant swine.
Screams on the Senate floor.
They should show him the door

He is the drama queen.
Treasonous.
Whining like a teen.
Drama queen.
Trump & Kav loving, you're obscene

July 1, Canada Day

Song Break: To the Canadian National Anthem

O Canada don't judge us by Don Trump.
We didn't vote for that ignorant chump.
With heavy hearts we apologize
For what he said of thee.
We get your point he's Putin's boy.
Installed by felony
O Canada we to wish to be Trump free.
O Canada please let us move to thee.
O Canada please let us move to thee.

Goodnight Poem

Goodnight Twitter. Goodnight Stars.
I wish Don was behind bars.
Stupid rallies every week.
Rambling racist Doublespeak.
Hate, hate, hate, his only themes.
Except for murderous regimes.
More of this Don? Heck no, screw it.
Resign like your buddy Pruitt.

Headline: Trump, at one of his hate-fest rallies, says he'd "like to test Elizabeth Warren's DNA" but that "he'd have to do so gently, because of MeToo".

Only vile racists say
They'd check opponent's DNA.
Only sexist fools like you
At a rally mock MeToo.
Stupid rallies on our dime.
Wasting money and our time.
Your tired litany of hate
Doesn't make the country great.
Putin and Kim aren't fine.
You hateful traitorous swine.

Song Break: To Neil Diamond's America

Czar. He's in bed with a czar.
His fat-clogged heart is as black as tar.
Tweet. All the garbage he'd tweet.
"Dear Leader's great," all the MAGA bleat.

There's a man with orange hair.
He's ruining America.
What's the truth, he doesn't care.
He's ruining America.
At a rally, in a tweet
He's ruining America.
Tweeting from his toilet seat.
He's ruining America.
He's ruining America.
Today!

A Poem for Scott Pruitt

EPA Scott had the real creepy notion
To corner the market on Ritz Carlton lotion.
Hands must be soft whatever the season.
When slept on used mattresses planning his treason.
But Scott, like any villain knows
No lotion, then he gets the hose.

Headline: July 3, 2018: Trump tweets that he's "a best-selling author" and "smarter than anyone", and complains that the media "pour" (not *pore*) over his tweets for mistakes.

I want a prez who knows how to spell.
Isn't a racist & won't rant or yell.
Who knows the diff. between poor, pour & pore.
Between they're & there & between your & you're.
Knows when to and not capitalize words.
Not tWeEt RanSoM Note-looking Donny turds.
One who is not as dumb as a stump.
One who is not inane Donald Trump.

Song Break: Sing Elvis (I Can't Help Falling in Love)

Wise men say: only fools Russian.
Trump can't help acting as Putin's boo.
Jail we pray: treason is a sin.
Trump can't help acting as Putin's boo.
Diarrhea flows, BS Donny tweets.
Muller knows hookers peed on sheets.
Jail his butt & his family too.
Trump can't help acting as Putin's boo.

Growing orange nose.
Each lie plain to see.
Everybody knows.
Trump means felony.
Wise men say: only fools Russian.
Trump can't help acting as Putin's boo.

Song Break: To Jackson Browne's Dr. My Eyes
(Dedicated to Ellie)

Donald the lying never ends.
In each tweet on Fox&Friends.
You are whining, I wish you would understand.
You're a lying, racist fool.
And an evil Russian tool.
Get resigning or they'll toss you on your can.

Donald the lies.
They will always fail.
You are unwise
To think you won't end up in jail.

Donald your giant orange rear
And your fishlike dopey sneer.
Tweeting, lying through your tiny orange hands.
You are evil and no good.
Impeach I wish they would.
No denying, just resign while you still can.

Donald the lies.
What's wrong in your brain?
No alibis.
In prison soon you will remain.

Goodnight Poem for "13 Angry Democrats"

Goodnight Twitter, goodnight, loon.
Trumpy whines the same old tune.
"No Collusion!", moron tweets.
(all the lies he just repeats).
Stow your "it's a Dem probe" Chubbs.
Mueller, Wray, & all: Repubs.
There's no "13 angry dems", you see
Just 10 complacent GOP.

Song Break: To Sing to "Lump"

Trump sat alone in a room with Vlad.
Said UK, NATO, and all allies are bad.
Tweets about Hillary for no reason.
Pays Nunes off to cover up his treason.
He's trump, he's trump, an epic fail.
He's trump, he's trump, belongs in jail.

Trump sat alone watching Fox TV.
Went down to Moscow to watch some hookers pee.
Kept tweeting Witch Hunt, No Collusion.
Who knew that Big Macs cause cognitive delusion.

He's trump, he's trump.
He's orange slime.
He's trump, he's trump.
He should do time.

Song Break: If You're Happy and You Know It

You're guilty and you know it, tiny hands.
You're guilty and you know it, tiny hands.
You're guilty and you know it.
Every tweet will only show it.
You're guilty and you know it tiny hands.

If you're guilty & you know it send 10 tweets.
Order Jeff to end the probe upon receipt.
Compare Paul M to Al Capone.
Admit your crimes via your phone.
If you're guilty & you know it send 10 tweets.

You're guilty and you know it, tiny hands.
You're guilty and you know it, tiny hands.
You're guilty and you know it.
Take that 'witch hunt' crap and stow it.
You're guilty and you know it, tiny hands.

Ode to the Whiner in Chief

You whine like a child.
Isn't it draining?
You live in denial.
Always complaining.
You whine about allies.
Whine 'bout the news.
You whine out your racist, ignorant views.
The Trump baby blimp? We should buy stock in it.
You fat whiny toddler
Who can't put a sock in it.

Song Break: Sing to The Banana Boat Song (Day-O)

Baio! Baio!
Prison should be Trump's only home.
Whiny orange, Putin's bum.
(Prison should be Trump's only home).
Keep on tweeting till Mueller come.
(Prison should be trump's only home).
Baio! Oh Scott Baio.
Prison should be trump's only home.

Headline July 2018: Trump, after the Helsinki
Summit with Putin, says Putin's "fine", and
"wouldn't interfere" with the election, despite what
our intelligence services found. Then, after
backlash, Trump backtracked, saying when he said
"wouldn't interfere" he meant "would".

Goodnight Twitter. Goodnight, bed.
Wish I was away instead
Of coming back to see Trump couldn't
Know the diff between would and wouldn't.
Or between poor, pour and pore.
Or between your and you're.
Gosh, my evening would be made
If Trump could pass the second grade.

Song Break: To Bonnie Tyler's Holding On For a Hero
(Dedicated to Tracy Smith)

Where have of Trump's men gone?
The lying, vile clods?
Felonies and guilty pleas.
Like Manafort, for fraud.
Mueller, be our white knight.
The country is in need.
Impeach, indict, remove that blight.
And we will all be freed.

Of Orange Nero.
Orange Nero and his vile alt-right.
A doddering fool.
Mar-a-Lard-Ass.
A blithering, blabbering blight.
The Orange Nero.
IQ is zero he is not too bright.
An old racist boor.
A raving mad loon.
His prison term should be for life.
Eighteen to life.

Headline: July 20, 2018: Michael Cohen reveals
that he taped his conversations with Don about
paying off porn stars:

Of all Donald's ethical scrapes.
Once again we expect sour grapes.
Seems Cohen was recording.
As Comey said, "Lordy",
Of the payment it seems there are tapes.

A Goodnight Poem

Goodnight Twitter, Goodnight, loon.
Grab your BabyTrump Balloon.
Mar-a-Lard-Ass must've felt down.
See his epic Twitter meltdown?
Maybe he just saw in court
Treason pal, Paul Manafort.
Trump can lie or bait Iran.
But Mueller h as a master plan.
Let the moron tweet his crap.
He won't beat the treason rap.

Song Break: To Bippity Boppity Boo

Orange & raving.
KFC craving.
Likely failed out of grade school.
Put em together & whadaya got?
Treasonous traitorous fool.
Dumb as bumpkin.
Color of pumpkin.
Foul as an IBS stool.
Put em together & whadaya got?
Treasonous traitorous fool.

Limericks for Manafort's Trial

Paul's trial and Donny is ranting.
While "lock him up" jurors be chanting.
Paul's guilty of treason.
And soon he'll have reason.
His pledge not to flip, be recanting.

Don will rant at his rally so manic.
But his wall request won't hide his panic.
Manafort faces prison.
For his treasonous vision.
They'll both go down like the Titanic.

And…a Bonus Poem

Today starts Paul Manafort's trial.
Donny is lost in denial.
Treasonous, traitorous, vile.
Spewing "hate immigrants" bile.
Tantrumming just like a child.
But, Donny, in just a short while
You'll be in jail breaking rock piles.

Song Break: To Goodbye Yellow Brick Road
(Dedicated to Beth Lanphere)

You are a fat orange clown.
You have childlike hands.
You should have stayed with the tsar.
You are a traitorous little man.
Many a better replacement.
For your regime could be found.
Merckel, Trudeau, or Macron
Or any fool wandering around.

Goodbye, fat orange load.
We're tired of hearing you howl.
Just go back to your penthouse.
Resign & throw in the towel.
Back to the gaudy apartment you keep.
Your glittering toilet of gold.
Oh America knows that a future lies
Beyond the fat orange load.

Morning, Twitter, morning, all.
Trump's up whining for his wall.
Guess MX's check got lost in post.
So at your rally, go and boast.
Have your rally, hate-fest slumming.
And lie through your teeth, but Mueller is coming.

A lawyer 'twas named Giuliani.
A ranting and lying old con he
Now spends all his time
Revealing the crimes
Of his traitorous client old Donnie.

Song Break: To The Beatles' Revolution

You tell me that there's no collusion.
Well you know.
Your lies are pretty bad.
Your victory was an illusion.
Well you know.
It was meddling by Vlad.
But when you say there's no obstruction,
Don't you know we're gonna vote you out.
Don't you know they're going to
Indict. Indict. Indict.

You tell me that there's no collusion.
Well, you know.
That is only in your head.
You're innocence is your delusion.
Well, you know.
You better cop a plea instead.
When you conspire with Russians day & night
All I can tell you is Donny they will indict.
Don't you know they're going to
Indict. Indict. Indict.

<u>Headline</u>: July 28, 2018, Don Jr.'s girlfriend, Kim Gargoyle, or whatever her name is, is booted from FoxNews for emailing naughty pictures to coworkers, likely of Fredo himself.

Goodnight Twitter what a week.
Jr.'s girlfriend seems did leak.
Pictures that are not so bonny
Trading pics of 'little Donny'.
And his dad is going ape.
Cause Mike Cohen said that there are tapes.
Tapes of crimes & tapes of bribes.
And all else that Cohen describes.
Donny boy, quite the fix in
Crime on tape you orange Nixon.

Song Break: To Let it Snow
(Dedicated to Nancy Hoffman)

Oh the GOP is so frightful.
Voting them out would be delightful.
The tantrums they like to throw.
Let em go, let em go let em go.

They are posters boys of alt-right
Racist hate, sexist lies are the norm.
Vote them out on election night.
The Blue Wave will be a storm.

The corruption they've been denying.
The past 10 years they've spent just lying.
Every year they reach a new low.
Let em go, let em go let em go.

<u>Headline</u>: July 28, 2018: Michael Cohen says that Trump (who lied again) knew in advance that Don Jr. planned to meet with Russia to get dirt on Hillary.

Goodnight all, expect rage tweeting.
Cohen: Don knew of the meeting.
Where Fredo met for dirt with Russians.
Now there will be repercussions
For your treason & your lies.
So a word to the unwise:
Tweet your tweets that makes no sense.
Mueller calls that "evidence".
Don there is but one deduction.
You are guilty of obstruction.

Song Break: To the 60's Hit "Tell Him"
I know something about Trump.
His butt is owned by Vlad.
And his witch hunt claim is a dud.
Mueller will get him.

If you want to be free of his orange hue
Round his coven up. Here's the thing to do:

Jail him cause the man committed treason.
Jail him for a million other reasons.
Jail him, jail him, jail him, jail him right now.

Ever since his term began
It seems that every man.
He hired was indicted.
Or they just plead guilty.
It's why to funerals he
So uninvited, oh yeah.

I know something about Trump.
He cannot shut his mouth.
Every tweet he lies & obstructs.
Oh Mueller get him.

If you want to be free of his orange hue
Round his witches up. Here's the thing to do:

Jail him, he's a lying orange traitor.
Jail him, he's a babbling dictator.
Jail him, jail him, jail him, jail him, right now.

Goodnight Poems

Goodnight Twitter. Goodnight, loon.
Now it seems the fat spittoon
Says Russia will soon interfere
To help the DEMOCRATS this year.
Donny dull & all amiss.
Putin's Junior Apprentice.
Want to stop the Russia hacking?
Your sanctions are the thing that's lacking.
Putin seeks to help you later.
So can it, you fat lying traitor.

Goodnight Twitter, Goodnight, loon.
Now the orange fat buffoon
Whining that the dems "resist".
Well here is what the moron missed:
We do, and will, with valid reason
Resist the traitor's constant treason.
So whine on, Don, tweet & screech.
But we don't stop till they impeach.

Song Break: To Act Naturally
(Dedicated to @NancyInTheWoods)

They went and put him in the White House.
Treason, he's complicit as can be.
Paul Manafort, the man who cowed to Russians.
But then the lout went and plead guilty.

Oh I bet you he's gonna be a big czar.
He hid his lies and spying so well.
He played his part, things would only worsen.
Oh Donny now you can go to hell.

So now Paul said he'll strike a deal with Mueller.
Trouble big, Don, you can plainly see.
Paul will lay out all of your collusion.
And all he had to do is plead guilty.

<u>Headline</u>: July 31, 2018: Manafort's trial begins.
So, of course, the orange moron holds another
taxpayer funded "there's no election but I need
MAGA rally" ego fest in Tampa, Florida.

Goodnight Twitter, ranty Grandpa.
Raving like a nut in Tampa.
Just another egofest
On our dime, because #BeBest.
Attacks again the Free Press
Ignores his Manafort-made mess.
But Donny, you can rant, attack
But you know you will not distract
Not tonight or any time
From your laundry list of crime.

Gather round & listen folks
The Mueller probe is not a "hoax".
Nor run by "angry dems", you see.
But by complacent GOP.
You can tweet your constant lies,
No collusion! Witch hunt! Spies!
Mueller's reads this drivel, trust us.
You're toast for obstructing justice.

Song Break: to Crosby Stills & Nash's Teach Your Children

You, you're a bloated load.
Built in that mode
Your health will fail now.
Eat that KFC
And you will see
Your heart will bail now.
Scarf the Big Mac and the Coke
But Donnie it's no joke.
Keep at it and you'll croak.
You Mar-a-Lard-Ass

Don, your orange rear
Gives children fear.
We want to know why.
You are so uncouth.
Can't speak the truth.
We wish you'd say "bye".
We should throw your butt in jail.
You raving epic fail.
Just tweet and rant and waiiiiilllll.
But we all hate you.

Headline: At his Tampa rally, Trump claims that you need an ID to buy groceries, and claims that because of him alone you can say "Merry Christmas". It's the middle July when he says this.

I cannot buy groceries without my ID.
Guess there'll be no fresh veggies for me.
Sure tariffs are putting us all out of business,
But thanks solely to Don I can say Merry Christmas!
They say its cultish to believe this old sap.
FoxNews-time is over, Don, time for you nap.

Song Break: To Walk This Way
(Dedicated to MYOB, @Mezzacrona66)

Lying & tweeting I'm a stupid orange fool.
With spray tan and ridiculous hair.
Tweetin' "No Collusion", raving in delusion.
Sitting round on my derriere.

When my wife did bore me
I hooked up with Stormy.
Then for cover and her silence I'd pay.
But trouble was a brewing
Mueller knew what he was doing.
Shoulda never fired Comey for Chris Wray

And the people say

Go away, oh Donny just go away.
Go away, oh Donny just go away.
Go away, Go away.
You will not be missed.

Headline: Trump, in a rally, announces he "loves England. They used to call it Great Britain. Now they call it the United Kingdom." Also, after critique from Lebron James, Trump sends a tweet or 10 bashing him.

I think that I shall never see
A man as stupid as DT.
A man who'd fit an XS mitten.
Who thinks England was called Great Britain.
Who thinks you need an ID for
Milk bought at the grocery store.
The dumbest man in history
Is Trump of course, no mystery.

There once was a moron named Don.
Who now is tweet-bashing Lebron.
While King James earned respect,
Trump, I suspect
Will soon to Fed prison be gone.

Is it just me who's sick to death
Of Dotard's weekly ego-fests?
Staged Klan rallies, spewing hate
Do not make our country great.
Attack the press, while praising Putin.
Orange traitor needs a bootin.
And all these rallies? On our dime.
The traitor should be doing time.

Headline: August 1, 2018: Trump tweets to Jeff
Sessions that he must end the Russia probe. Also,
he bizarrely compared the Manafort trial to charges
against Al Capone.

Goodnight Twitter. Goodnight, loon.
Now the orange fat buffoon
Spent the day in crime by phone.
Said Paul M's like Al Capone.
Obstructed justice yet again.
Tweeting Russia probe must end.
Ordered Jeff to do the act.
Mueller noticed, that's a fact.
And Don copped to the Russia meeting.
Guilty plea via his tweeting.

<u>Headline</u>: Trump announces the creation of his
"Space Force".

Goodnight Twitter Goodnight, loon.
Oh the ever-golfing goon
Wants to put troops into space.
To try save his orange face.
No dispute, Don, no rebuttal
We'll put you on the maiden shuttle.
If you don't end up behind bars.
You'll be the first con sent to Mars.

Song Break: To Stairway to Heaven

There's a traitor I know.
And his hair's painted gold.
And he has an IQ of 11.
When the Russia probe's closed.
All his lies are exposed.
And he'll be thrown in jail & be done for.

He still bleats for his wall.
He's an ignorant bore.
Racist, a lout & demeaning.
Just an old racist crook.
And brain dead by the look
As all of his tweets have no meaning.

Oooh and he has an IQ of 11.

: In response to the California wildfires,
Trump, in 3 separate tweets, blames the State,
saying it is "diverting" water into the ocean. He's
referring to the fact that water flows downhill from
the mountains.

Goodnight Twitter. Goodnight, loon.
Now the orange raving goon
Thrice tweeted the crazy notion
CA put water in the ocean.
Where's the moron get this crap?
It's well past time for his nap.
He will need a babysitter.
To stop confessing crimes on Twitter.
So moron just tweet on
Soon to jail you will be gone.

Song Break: Return to Sender

Racist, orange & bloated
A stupid lying sack.
He was installed by Putin.
I'd like to send him back.
(the rotten dotard)
Return to sender.
He's Putin's own.
Send the bill to Michael Cohen.
Return to sender.
Election hacked.
Sent him to Russia
But the moron kept coming back.

<u>Headline</u>: After months of calling it "fake news",
Trump admits that Don Jr. met with Russians for
the express purpose of getting dirt on Hillary, and
not, as Jr. testified before Congress, about
"adoptions."

Goodnight Twitter. Goodnight, loon.
Now the orange hued maroon
In a new tweet now confessed
Traitor Tot lied to Congress.
Says the little lying dude
Met with Russia to collude.
No adoption lie this time
Just admitted to the crime.
Won't be fake news television
When the pair is put in prison.

Headline: Trump announces he is ending the
decades-old ban on importing asbestos into the US
and declares asbestos "safe." Why? Because,
surprise, surprise, Russia is the only exporter. Also,
Don's face adorns the Russian palettes of asbestos
to be shipped. Sadly, I'm not kidding. Go Google it,
I'll wait....

Goodnight Twitter. Goodnight, loon.
Now Russia-loving goon wants to bring asbestos
back
Cause Putin told him "stay on track".
You see, it's Russia's big export.
So watch Don lie and distort.
You think it's safe, Don, know so well?
Let's use it in your prison cell.

: August 19, 2018: Rudy Giuliani gives a
TV interview admitting Fredo's meeting at Trump
Tower was to get for dirt on Hillary, not adoption as
claimed, and says, of the lie, "truth isn't truth." Yup,
those were his exact words. Truth isn't truth.

Goodnight Twitter how uncouth.
Rudy says truth isn't truth.
Don attacks the NY Times
For reporting on his crimes.
Every vile criminal deed
The "fake news" is his Twitter feed.
Rudy gave another option
Said meeting was not for adoption.
Real news, oh it will excite
When Team Treason they indict.

Song Break: The Doors Light My Fire

Every word you say's untrue.
You're nothing but an orange liar.
But Mueller he is on to you.
Donny, Donny pants on fire.
Mueller knows you did conspire.
Mueller knows you did conspire.
Michael Cohen, he wore a wire!

Headline: Trump's military parade is cancelled over excessive cost. Trump also complains that his right-wing shills were "shadow banned" and "silenced" on social media. The shills tweet the same thing, meaning, they were obviously not banned.

Goodnight Twitter. Goodnight, loon.
Now the orange Kim Jong Un
Is losing his mind, all afraid
Cause he can't have his parade.
Rants of Twitter "shadow bans".
Guess he lost himself some fans.
On a rant about the news.
Says media bans right-wing views.
But the media's awash
In right-wing hate, lies & hogwash.
It's Trump who oft bans CNN
Calls it and others "fake" again.
Don could not be any denser
As it's him who tries to censor.

Song Break: To Jackson 5's ABC

KFC.
You know that it's all he'll eat.
Oh greasy food can't be beat.
KFC
Buy 10 wings and you get one free!
Come on, come on so he can carry out.

Song Break: To My Bonny

My Donny committed obstruction.
My Donny commits felonies.
Oh Donny is going to prison.
So say hi to Paulie for me.
Say hi, say hi, say hi to
Paulie for me, for me!

Oh Donny caused quite the commotion
In Moscow to watch hookers pee.
Now Don will need Scott Pruitt's lotion.
He's going to prison you see.
Big Macs! Big Macs!
No Big Macs in prison for thee.

Headline: A man with a pickaxe destroys Trump's star on the Walk of Fame. The people who maintain the Walk announce they will not replace the star, because they know it will just get destroyed again, and Don had paid to have it installed to begin with (versus having it dedicated to him).

Moron's star will be gone from the walk of fame.
Vandals and CA aren't to blame.
But his sexism, and being a racist
His stupid lies, hateful & basest.
He'll blame Dems all that they're in with
He had to buy his own star to begin with.
A blow to his ego, as fragile as glass.
That's what you get, Don, you ignorant ass.

Song Break: To Sooner or Later Love is Gonna Get You

Sooner or later Mueller's gonna get you.
You orange traitor, it is a given.
It's just a matter of time
Before you pay for your crime.
The Russian ties you've been hiding.
It's just a question of when
You'll end up in the Pen.
No use whining & lying.
Sooner or later Mueller's gonna get you…

Song Break: To House of the Rising Sun

There is a man in old DC
They call the lying Don.
He is the ruin of all he'd touch.
Can't wait till he is gone.

"Oh Mother", cried Pence-y
"Spank me on rump
I spent my life in sin and misery
Bowing down to the traitor Trump".

Song Break: I Want to Hold Your Hand

Oh I'll tell you something
You angry orange man.
When I say that something.
You have tiny hands.
Oh you have tiny hands.
Oh you have tiny hands.
And when I see you I get nauseous inside.
You're so revolting and we know.
That you lied!
That you lied!
That you lied!

Song Break: Old Macdonald

Old fat Donald had a talk.
E-I-E-I-O.
Repeating the same BS squawk.
E-I-E-I-O.
With a fake news here, no collusion there.
Here a lie, there a lie.
Here some orange hair dye.
Old fat Donald had a talk.
E-I-E-I-O.

Old fat Donald lied you see.
E-I-E-I-O.
He paid to watch some hookers pee.
E-I-E-I-O.
There's collusion here & obstruction there.
Here a crime, there a crime.
Donny's gonna' do time.
Old fat Donald lied you see.
E-I-E-I-O.

Old fat Donald had a phone.
E-I-E-I-O.
Plotted crimes with Roger Stone.
E-I-E-I-O.
A hacked email here, texts of meetings there.
Evidence, evidence.
We'll be stuck with Mike Pence?
Old fat Donald had a phone.
E-I-E-I-O.

Song Break In honor of Aretha Franklin

C-O-N-V-I-C-T!
Treason is a felony.
C-O-N-V-I-C-T!
Witch hunt? Guilty plea.
(Oh lock up Donny, lock up Donny, lock up
Donny...)

Song Break: To Mr. Grinch

You're a mean one Mr. Trump.
A fat & bloated load.
You're as orange as kumquat, as slimy as a toad.
Mr. Trump.
You're an ignorant despot.
With tiny doll hands.

<u>Headline</u>: August 30, 2018. He holds yet another
rally.

Another rally of the Klan.
For the lying orange man.
Hours of hate, hours of lies.
Attacks FBI as democrat spies.
"Witch Hunt!" "No Collusion!" that'll be certain.
"Pay no mind to Don's Iron Curtain".
God, if you'd like to show justice as proof
Go Old Testament, and on them drop a roof.

Headline: August 27, 2018. The orange idiot raises
flag to full staff to attack McCain one day after he
died.

Goodnight Twitter his & hers.
Draft-dodging Captain Bone Spurs
Flew flag full staff to show disdain.
As if any doubt remained.
He is a coward, traitor bred.
Loyal just to Russian red.
This vile crooked lying thief
Should not be Commander in Chief.
The only things that Don commands
Are his tiny orange hands.

: September 4 – Don calls Bob Woodward
a liar.

Woodard v Trump a battle of fact.
Prize-winning author & B-lister act.
The man who brought down Tricky Dick.
And a bumbling fool who is kindly called thick.
A man who won the Pulitzer Prize.
An orange dolt who always lies.
Don your mouth should be shut.
For Woodward he will kick your orange butt.

<u>Headline</u>: August 29, 2018 - Trump threatens to "regulate" Google, claims it is "rigged" because he searched his name and found mean entries and "not all the good he's done".

There once was a fat orange liar.
With Russia he did conspire.
Said Google was "rigged".
Cause search "traitorous pig",
And you get Don with his pacifier.

Donny, obese orange-wigged.
Now says Goggle is rigged.
When he searched for his name
The results were the same:
Traitorous treasonous fool.
Likely he flunked out of school.
History, law, English failed.
But soon the fat crook will be jailed.

Goodnight Twitter. Goodnight, loon.
Now the free speech hating goon
Says Google's rigged, and the reason?
You google "Trump", and you get "treason".
Other "Don" search that he found:
Traitor, dimwit, racist, clown.
Google isn't rigged, you mess.
It's that you're all those things and less.

<u>Headline</u>: 9/11/18: Trump, ahead of Hurricane Florence, warned America that the hurricane is "very wet and very big." This, after last year stating that Puerto Rico was an island "surrounded by water, big water." (I'm not kidding about either quote - Google, it. Go ahead, I'll wait....)

I think that I shall never see
A man as stupid as DT.
A man who in his dumbest yet
Reminds us hurricanes are wet.
A man with orange face and hair.
And like a storm, full of hot air.
For once he speaks from whence he knows.
For, like a hurricane, he blows.

Song Break: To Take Good Care of My Baby

You're a fat orange baby.
Tweet stuff no one understands.
You need a full time coddler.
You're like a cranky toddler.
Except with much, much smaller hands.

You're a fat orange baby.
You just whine & moan and wail.
But Mueller discover.
The crimes you tried to cover.
And then Donny it's off to jail

Headline: Despite sworn testimony that he attempted to rape Dr. Christine Blasey Ford, despite multiple proved lies under oath to Congress, and despite the American Bar Association revoking its recommendation of his confirmation, Mitch McConnell, Orin Hatch, and Lindsey Graham vow to "plow through" to confirm "Bart O Kavanaugh" to the Supreme Court.

Poems for the Worst SCOTUS Hearing Ever

So, you applied for a GOP job.
You gang raped, you shouted and raged like a slob.
Boofing & drunk, a druggy the highest.
Racist, unhinged, and off-the-charts biased.
Lied & obstruct, covered up & conspired.
So of course GOP said, "Welcome, you're hired"

I do not like that Lindsey Graham.
I do not like him, Sam I Am.
I do not like that Chuck Grassley.
Gaseous bag of felony.
I do not like that Orin Hatch.
Whose evil only trump can match.
I do not like the GOP.
Vote them out won't you, for me?

: Susan Collins, the supposed moderate, votes to confirm Kavanaugh in a one-hour speech attacking the rape victims for speaking out against him.

I do not like Susan Collins of Maine.
I think there is something wrong with her brain.
I did not like her long, rambling speech.
Her blaming the victims in partisan screech.
I would not like this old jerk anywhere.
I hope she is eaten by a large grizzly bear.

Song Break: To Wake Up Little Suzie

Wake up little Suzie, wake up.
Wake up little Suzie, wake up.
Ignored the rape victims' shout.
You stupid NRA lout.
You sycophant, you party shill.
I hope they vote your ass out.
Wake up little Suzie.
Wake up little Suzie.
They'll send your ass home.

Wake up little Suzie, wake up
Wake up little Suzie wake up
You fell for Kavanaugh's plot
He's Russian paid, Russian bought
You evil tool, you vile fool
You simpering, feckless old (person)
Wake up little Suzie
Wake up little Suzie
They'll send your ass home.

A Trio of Limericks

There once was a fat orange cretin.
Who spent day & night just rage-tweetin'.
But Mueller sees all.
T'will be Don's downfall.
And at trial he will take a beatin'.

Each night trump rage tweets like a toddler.
And his drivel grows odder and odder.
But it would be sweet.
If Bob M read each tweet.
They're obstruction of evidence fodder.

Trump's seeing the trouble that he's in.
All of us well know the reason.
He'll whine and complain.
But the fact will remain.
They'll impeach come the autumnal season.

Song Break: To American Pie
(Dedicated to @MomThoughts)

A long, long time ago,
I can still remember
When our president wasn't so senile.
Now every time Don gets the chance
Surrounds himself with sycophants.
With nazis, traitors, criminals most vile.
Every speech that he'd deliver
Is foul like his cirrhotic liver.
But, we must remember.
Election Day's November.
The sweet sound of the MAGA shout
When we can vote the traitors out.
Be celebrations all about.
The day we nail this guy.
Bye, bye Russian sycophant spy.
See you later, orange traitor.
We are sick of your lies.
All the guilty pleas,
Everything you touch dies.
Next election, traitor Trump say goodbye.

Headline - Omorosa released her book. Trump goes
even more insane, calling her "low IQ" and
claiming she signed a non-disclosure agreement.

Goodnight Twitter, what a day.
Omorosa signed an NDA?
So she slept with Donny too?
Deary, what is wrong with you?
I bet the 1st line Donny taught her.
"You remind me of my daughter."
The line that makes porn stars hearts melt.
But staffers, grab your chastity belt.

Headline. – The "alt-right" plans another rally in Charlottesville, VA on the anniversary of the march the prior year where Heather Heyer was killed.

Dear Nazis:

We do not want you in DC.
We don't want hatred, don't you see?
Just stay on your mommy's porch.
And stow your little tiki torch.
We do not want to hear you chant.
To whine your slogans, hate and rant.
We all want to see you fail.
Your next march should be right to jail.

Song Break! To Help
Written by @ToddFaber

When I was younger, so much younger than today.
I didn't have to pander to the mob or KKK.
When I hear Mueller's name I'm not so self-assured.
Cause all I've done is rant & moan.
And handle Putin's chores.

Watch me everyone I'm going down.
And I don't appreciate those who are brown.
Help me get my golf spikes off the ground.
Oh Rudy, please, please help me.

<u>Headline</u>: Manafort pleads guilty.

Goodnight Twitter. Goodnight, loon.
What a field day for the loon.
Paul pleaded guilty to his lying.
And as well to Russian spying.
"Foreign agent, I" said he.
Know what, Don of Felony?
When he talks, & Coheny too.
It is MuellerTime for you.

Headline: Stormy Daniels releases here memoir, and writes that Trump's penis reminds her of "Toad from Mario Kart", covered in "yeti" hair.

Goodnight Donny, bloated load.
Or shall I call you Tiny Toad.
Oh for all your vile meanness.
Seems you have a micro-penis.
Atop Stormy, grunting, sweaty.
Like, she said, an orange yeti.
Imagine the horror and hysterics.
If you fathered 3 more Eric's.

Finally, Song Break: One I cannot wait to sing
To The Everly Brothers' Bye-Bye Love
(Dedicated to @TheRynHeart)

There goes fat baby.
He did collude.
He's been indicted.
Oh Don, you're screwed.
Committed treason.
It is a sin.
Now Mueller caught you.
You'll never win.

Bye-bye Trump.
Bye-bye treasonous.
Hello, prison dress.
Mueller knows you lied.
Bye traitor Trump, bye-bye.

No more "a with hunt!"
No BS tale.
You've be indicted.
You orange whale.
And here's the reason
We'll all be free.
You'll be indicted.
Of felonies.

Bye-bye Trump.
Bye-bye treasonous.
Hello, prison dress.
Mueller knows you lied.
Bye traitor Trump, bye-bye.

Acknowledgments

Thank you to Mom and Dad. Words cannot express how much your love, support, intellect, talent, and humor mean to me. I love you both more than anything in this world.

Thank you Barney the Golden Doodle, for not eating the proof of this book. Good boy!

Thank you once again to Mark Plavin for creating the cover art for this book and for being my best friend and 'older brother' by 3 days since we were kids.

Thank you to all of you on Twitter who encouraged me, laughed with me, and battled trolls with me. Thank you Sam, Ryn, Boston, Dani, April, Kay, and Nicki, for your kindness, and for being the 'test audience' for many of these songs. You are the best tweeps a fella' could hope for.

Howard Altman
October 2018

Made in the USA
San Bernardino, CA
15 November 2018